The Book of Horses

The Book of
HORSES

DORIAN WILLIAMS

J. B. LIPPINCOTT COMPANY, PHILADELPHIA AND NEW YORK

First published 1971 in the United States of America
by J. B. Lippincott Company
Library of Congress Catalog Card No 70–164107

Second printing

Printed in Hong Kong by
Leefung-Àsco Printers Limited

ISBN 0–397–00888–0

Contents

Acknowledgment

The Author and Publishers wish to thank the following for permission to reproduce the illustrations included in this book:
J. Allan Cash, fig 12; Camera Clix, figs 1 and 60; R. Coleman of Baron Studios Limited, figs 63, 96, 102 and 112; J. Findlay Davidson, figs 2, 3, 4, 6, 7, 13, 16, 20, 21, 22, 23, 24, 28, 35, 36, 40, 43, 44, 47, 48, 62, 65, 68, 69, 70, 71, 72, 74, 75, 77, 78, 79, 80, 84, 85, 89, 92, 94, 99, 103 and 104; Fox Photos Limited, fig 52; Noel Habgood, fig 59; De Vere Helfrich, fig 111; Pam Howlett, figs 52, 54, 55, 86, 108 and 109; *Hoofs & Horns* and K. Steven, figs 82, 83 and 85; Hulton Press Limited, fig 91; Keystone Press Agency, fig 101; R. Löbl, fig 53; Frank H. Meads, figs 106 and 107; Nicholas Meyjes, figs 4, 14, 15, 18, 25, 32, 34, 35, 37, 38, 41, 42, 45, 46, 49, 50, 67, 69, 73, 76, 87 and 90; Miles Brothers, fig 100; Monty, figs 10 and 27; John Nestle, fig 26; M. A. E. Pocock, figs 11, 30, 31, 33, 51, 64, 105 and 110; Paul Popper, fig 29; *Radio Times* Hulton Picture Library, fig 95; the Rodeo Information Commission, figs 113, 114 and 115; W. W. Rouch & Co. Limited, fig 97; H. Smith, fig 8; Sport & General, figs 17 and 19; Elisabeth Weiland, figs 56, 57, 58, 59, 61, 65 and 66; Winants Brothers, fig 98.

Introduction

Regretfully one has to accept the fact that the horse today is a luxury. With very few exceptions the horse is no longer essential in any aspect of life. And yet, paradoxically, the horse is more popular than ever before. There are more horses in training for racing, there are more show jumpers, there are more horses and ponies being bred than at any time in the past. Driving horse-drawn vehicles is becoming extraordinarily popular again. There are more children and young people – and not so young people – in Pony Clubs and Riding Clubs than at any time since these organisations were founded. More people are riding to hounds. More people are playing polo, and far more people are taking part in One Day and Three Day Events than when the first Three Day Event was held at Badminton in 1949.

Pony trekking, pack trips and trail riding are popular pastimes. Riding Schools have mushroomed in the last ten years. In point-to-points, as in race meetings, the entries are often so big that races have to be run in two or three sections. More people are seriously interested in dressage than would have been believed possible when it was first introduced in the late thirties.

How can all this be explained? Why is it that today, when man can fly to the moon and walk on it – and perhaps before the end of the century will be able to ride on it! – millions of people should be so interested in a form of transport that was part of the way of life before cars and aeroplanes were ever thought of?

The answer probably lies firstly in people's great desire to preserve the past, to recapture the 'good old days'. Although after World War I the horse was becoming obsolete and even more so after World War II, people were determined not to give up riding. It reminded them of the peaceful days of the past, it was a reaction to the hustle and bustle, the noise and speed of modern times. How nice it was to proceed at a speed considerably more sedate than the speed at which one travelled in a car or a train or an aeroplane. Yet at the same time one could enjoy all the sensation of speed and excitement, for to the rider a horse galloping at twenty miles an hour seems just as fast as sixty miles an hour to a driver, or six hundred miles an hour to a pilot.

So it is that against all odds the horse has survived, in the industrialised world, right up to the last quarter of the twentieth century. To countless thousands of people it still gives enormous pleasure.

1 *A good-looking half-breed, still in use between shafts*

The Working Horse

As a working animal the horse has barely survived. Although it has not entirely disappeared from the jobs with which it was so long associated, the working horse nowadays is very much a rarity.

The Coster (a horse-drawn street vendor) is still to be seen in city streets, as is the odd delivery cart. In eastern England and in Europe, the horse-drawn farm vehicle (2, 3) is still used – and how well such working horses can look (1). Horses also continue to be indispensible for cattle-ranching and sheep-farming in the United States and Australia, and are still sometimes used for this purpose in England (4).

2 *The heavy horse can still be seen on the farm*

3 *A heavy horse at work in France*

Horses are still invaluable on sheep-farms

5 *The Sherry horses in all their glory at a fiesta*

6, 7
A Spanish
Sherry hors
headpiece a
tailpiece

14

9 *The famous French-bred Percheron*

8 *The great Shire, nowadays increasingly popular in America*

The heavy horse is a real rarity. Fortunately, however, the big breweries still use these magnificent animals (many of which weigh as much as a ton), as much for publicity purposes as for their basic purpose – that is as a means of locomotion. And in many parts of the world, farm horses can be seen in use, pulling the plough or the hay wagon (8, 9, 12).

Twenty years ago there were in England over 20,000 ponies used in the coal pits. Now, to everyone's relief, although they have always been wonderfully well treated – indeed they have been the pride of those who looked after them – they are on the way out, and soon they will have disappeared altogether from the pits and their jobs done by up-to-date machinery (14).

More and more horses and ponies are being used between the shafts for recreational purposes. Driving has recently become very popular (16), and surely there is nothing more elegant than a smart turnout with a team of horses or ponies, or a smart high-stepping hackney. There is always a fascination about harness and people will always love driving – even though it is not easy today on the public roads which call for exceptional skill on the part of the driver and a perfect temperament in the horse or pony between the shafts (15, 18).

In many countries harness is used as an opportunity for decoration. The famous Clydesdales in Scotland are a wonderful sight at the Royal Highland Show, as are the teams of heavy horses at Toronto's Royal Winter Fair; so too are the famous Sherry horses from Jerez, even their tails being decorated (5, 6, 7). Displays at shows all over the world, at which the driver and passengers wear the clothes worn in the hey-day of the horse, are extremely elegant and evoke the past in a most dramatic way (10, 11). At the same time horse-drawn vehicles are still put to more practical purposes in many countries, such as Germany, Switzerland, Austria, where on the big

10 *Old-world elegance*

11 A scene from yesterday in South Africa today

estates they are used for driving round the grounds, with the grooms often still wearing the landlord's livery – so preserving yet again a link with the past.

Nor should one forget those riders who ride in livery or uniform every day of their working lives. I am referring to the mounted police officers all over the world who do such a wonderful job in controlling crowds, restoring order, or simply adding to the pageantry of an occasion (13, 17, 19).

12 The common cart-horse – but worth his weight in gold

13 Canadian Mounties – spectacular but efficient

14 The last of the Pit ponies

15 Old-world use of harness ponies

16 H.R.H. The Duke of Edinburgh driving the Queen's team of crossbred Cleveland Bay geldings through a water hazard at the 1973 European Driving Championships

17 One of London's famous mounties meets an East-end Coster pony

14

REFRESHMENT

19 *A less romantic use of the police horse*

Police horses, of course, go through a very thorough training which prepares them for every sort of eventuality. But one never fails to be lost in admiration for their patience and their kind, placid temperament in face of situations which are often ugly and even dangerous.

18 *The Hackney, increasingly popular*

20 Sunday morning in an English village

Riding

It is difficult to assess how many people ride in the world, or indeed in any one country. It is estimated that perhaps as many as half a million people ride in Britain, or one in every five hundred. In California the proportion is roughly the same; in most European countries it is somewhat lower, except in Germany where the proportion is even higher than in California or Britain.

The Pony Club has expanded rapidly throughout the world: in Britain there are now three hundred branches with thirty thousand members, while Australia has almost five hundred branches and a membership almost as large as Britain's. There is also rapid expansion in the United States and Canada where there are now close on two hundred branches.

Riding is now a regular pastime, not only for people who live in the country, but also for people who live in the suburbs (20). There are nearly three hundred Riding Clubs in Britain where members receive regular instruction at weekends (21). Many of these become professional enough to take part in displays, appearing even at such occasions at the famous Horse of the Year Show in London (22).

21 *Riding Club receiving instruction*

22 Riding Club in glamorous guise: performing a quadrille at the Horse of the Year Show in London

23 *Dressage, or haute école – the ultimate riding skill: Dr Reiner Klinke on Mehuned*

One of the joys of riding is that it can be enjoyed at any level. If one is interested in equitation one can take it very seriously and become accomplished at dressage, known as haute école (23). At an only slightly lower level one can enjoy showing, where the emphasis is on conformation, appearance, turn-out and performance – and how elegant these turn-outs can look (24, 25, 26, 27) and how beautifully the horse and ponies are ridden. It is here that a standard is set to which many will want to aspire – a standard which is well within the scope of ordinary people if they are determined enough, even though anything but elementary dressage may be a bit beyond them.

It is not always the show ring, of course; the majority of people get their pleasure from everyday hacking or from going for rides in the country. On a fine day this can be an incomparable pastime – but even on a bad day it is fun, because for the enthusiast riding is always a pleasure (28).

It is almost true to say that riding can be enjoyed at any age. One is never too young to start, though I am sure that one should not expect a child to take it too seriously too young. A very quiet pony, or even a donkey on which a child can just ride about happily and unworried is ideal (30).

But one can also ride until late in life. Many people have still been riding beyond eighty, but it is probably best if the horse is fairly old too, being more sensible. The gentleman in the picture (31) and his horse add up between them to a hundred years.

However seriously one takes one's riding, one should always remember that first and foremost riding should be fun, something to be enjoyed (29).

25 Elegance in the show-ring

24 Showing – the weight-carrying cob

27 *Champion pony*

28 Riding for fun

29 You could hardly help enjoying riding in Colorado

30 You are never too young to put up a good show . . .

31 . . . nor too old: between them, this horse and rider have lived for a hundred years

Ponies

Although the horse as we know it today is descended from a much smaller animal that ran about the desert a million years ago, the development of the pony as such is of comparatively recent origin.

The pony in its native state is still very wild-looking, now that we are so used to ponies being trimmed and groomed and even clipped; but thanks to the temperament of most breeds it does not take very long to tame a wild pony and make him usable.

As we have mentioned earlier, ponies and riding have never been more popular. At weekends one is almost certain to see a party of riders out any morning in any village; but for many it is the pony in its natural state or the pony in hand that, from the aesthetic point of view, gives the greatest pleasure.

Of all the countries in the world, Britain is particularly fortunate in its large number of indigenous breeds. The ponies of the British Isles are all equally famous (throughout the world) and practical in their different ways. The Connemara (32) is wonderfully strong and many well-known horses as well as ponies are descended from Connemaras. The Welsh are elegant, beautiful movers and have lovely temperaments (33, 35, 36). They have become very popular in the United States for both riding and driving.

The Dartmoor (37, 39) is a friendly little pony, hardy, having lived for centuries on Dartmoor, used to people, and ideal for children. From Somerset and Devon come the Exmoor, recognizable from their mealy muzzle (34). They, too, are hardy and well suited to children. The New Forest (38) is perhaps the most famous and well-loved of all the ponies, known to thousands who drive through this region of Britain. These three breeds are popular in Canada, but virtually unknown in the United States.

In the North of England are the Fell, and the not dissimilar Dale. Each is a great weight-carrier despite its small size and is as often ridden by adults as by children (40, 41, 43). The smallest pony in the British Isles is, of course, the Shetland (42). He is stronger than a good many people think and is a real little character. The Shetland is very sure-footed and is usually docile and so loved by small children. There is a lot of Shetland breeding in the US, where they are also driven by adults in the show ring, hitched to an elegant viceroy.

Finally there is the Highland: as strong as a horse in many respects, it is very sure-footed and is in regular use in the Highlands both as a working and as a riding pony (45).

The Palomino is not, as is sometimes thought, a breed. Rather it is a colour, and it is in fact possible to have a palomino, with its lovely cream mane and tail, in any breed (44).

33 Welsh Pony stallion

34 (left)
Young Exmo

35 Wel
Mountain
stallion

36 Welsh Mountain in action

Though the pony is far more common in Britain than elsewhere, lovely ponies are to be found in other countries such as Norway (46) and Austria, where one has the Haflinger with its astonishing mane (49).

Increasingly British ponies are being exported to other countries, not least to the United States. Only a few years ago children in many countries who wanted to learn to ride had to wait until they were old enough to ride a horse; now ponies are available. At the same time some experts are of the opinion that people are likely to ride better if they have only learnt on a horse and not a pony. In their view, the two are so different that people who have learnt to ride on a pony find it too difficult to transfer to a horse: or, alternatively, learn bad habits riding a pony which make them bad riders when they come to horses.

One cannot help feeling, however, that any child is extremely fortunate to have ridden when very small in leading rein classes (47) or in gymkhanas (48, 50), which make a rider wonderfully active and supple, or to have enjoyed the wide open spaces and sunshine of California, Australia, New Zealand or South Africa (51).

Pony sales, in some countries known as Fairs, are still held all over the world. As a rule ponies are brought into these sales unbroken and can be bought quite cheaply (52). Many of these Sales are very good, but some are undesirable, selling ponies that are in pitiful condition. Certainly one can get a really good bargain at a sale; but one can also, only too easily, buy a pig in a poke. The important thing to remember is that these ponies are often very young and should not be ridden until they are properly grown, at three or four years old.

38 New Forest ponies in their natural surroundings

37 Dartmoor ponies in their native habitat

39 Dartmoor stallion

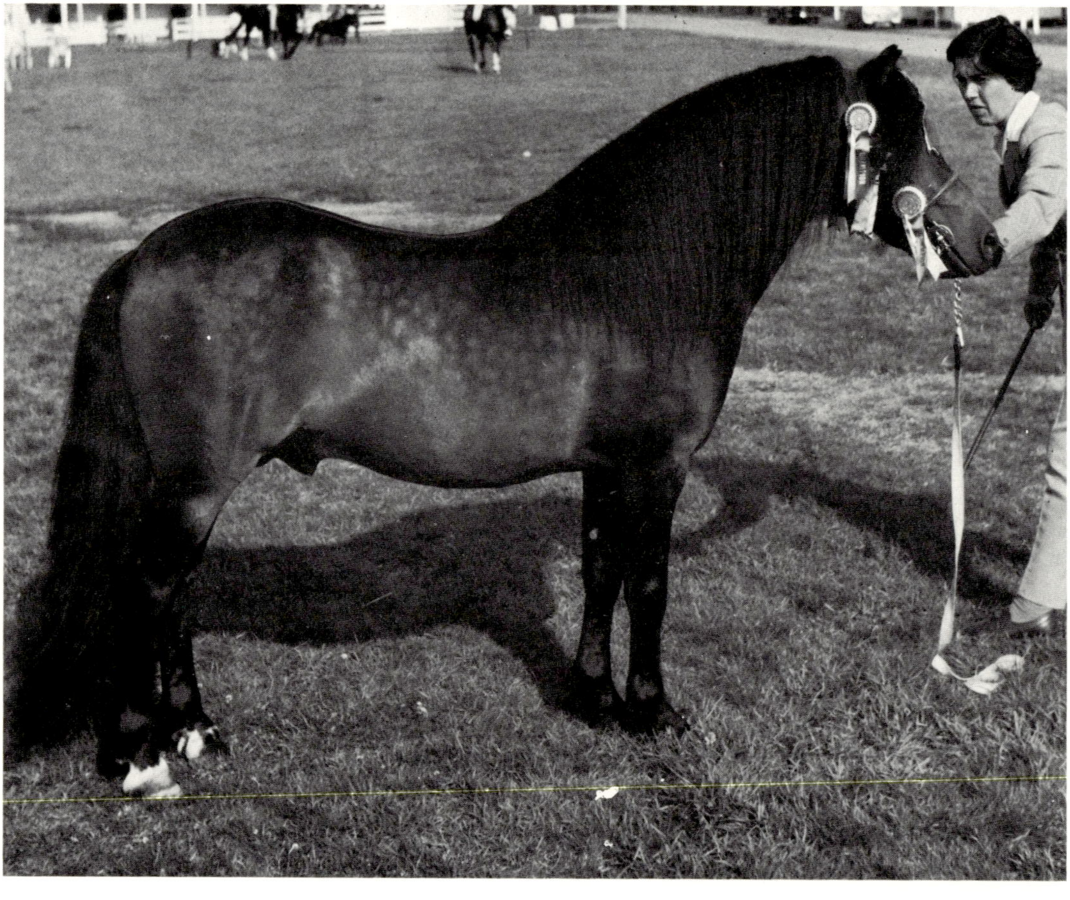

40 *A Champion Fell Pony*

41 (left) Fell mare

42 The ever-popul Shetland

43 A Champion Dale Pony

44 Beautiful Palomino heads

45 *Highland ponies*

46 *Norwegian ponies*

47 *Beginners only: a leading-rein class*

49 (left)
The Haflinger

50 *Mounted Games*

51 *Wide open spaces in South Africa*

52 *A Pony Sale*

53 A lovely young colt

Studs

It is not surprising that the world over there has been a marked increase in the number of studs of both ponies and thoroughbreds. The latter, of course, can be very profitable, while pony studs always give great satisfaction, and in a few cases make money.

The very sight of a mare and foal is a delight, but this is nothing compared with the satisfaction and excitement of owning a mare which presents you with a lovely foal. Within hours, minutes almost, a new-born foal (54) is on its feet, all gangly, a little wobbly, but actually capable of cantering. Within days it is strong and healthy and very handsome (55). Week by week one can watch it growing

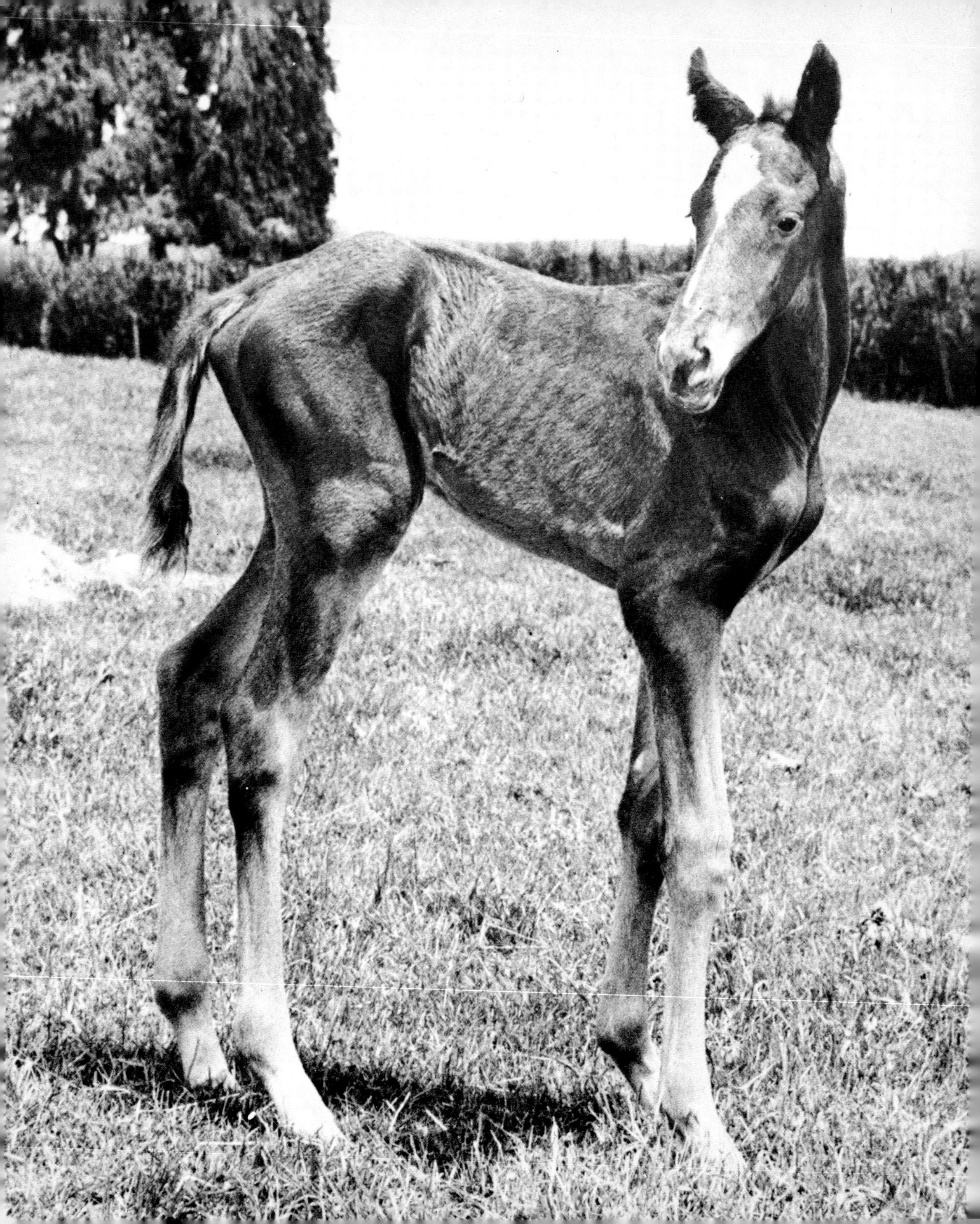

into a fine colt (53) or an attractive filly (56), soon big enough and independent enough to join the 'gang', the mares and foals, colts and fillies that make such a lovely picture at any stud – whether it be in Britain, the United States (60), Europe (57), or indeed anywhere else (58).

It is easy to understand why the great artist George Stubbs loved more than anything to paint mares and foals, youngstock out in their paddocks, with the lush grass beneath their feet and the green trees behind them. In the same way the cameraman loves to capture these beautiful scenes. The magnificent opportunities he has are illustrated by the lovely pictures from Germany and Switzerland (59, 61). But no less attractive studies could come from Kentucky or Western Australia, from Norway or Capetown.

Or Piba: for Piba is where, perhaps, the best known of all stallions are bred – the magnificent Lippizaners (62). Transported from Spain over four hundred years ago, they have now for centuries occupied this famous stud and provided the world-famous Spanish Riding School in the heart of Vienna, with its gilt and crimson, its exquisite chandeliers, its impressive gallery and Royal Box.

How superb the stallions look in their brilliant quadrille, their riders still in their smart eighteenth-century livery, performing to the accompaniment of the soft music. Is it surprising that these stallions are so proud?

The thoroughbred stallion is, of course, the most valuable horse in the world. Nijinsky (102) has just been valued at two-and-a-half million pounds. After a successful racing career a top-class stallion like Nijinsky or Royal Palace (63) goes to stud. What a long way the thoroughbred has come from the little Arab stallion first imported to Europe six hundred years ago, from which every stallion in the world has descended.

55. *A week old now*

56 *Arab mare and foal*

57 Posing for the camera – French mares and foals

58 Arabs and Barbs in Tunisia

60 Colts on an American ranch, waiting to be broken in

59 The peaceful paddock

61 A spacious stud in Switzerland

62 *Lippizaner stallion at the Spanish Riding School, Vienna*

Naturally stallions, and indeed all horses, vary a little in their characteristics according to the country from which they come. Some are much bigger and stronger than others; others more active; they come too in different colours. But they are all superb to look at. It is no exaggeration to say that the stallion, with the lion, is the most handsome animal in the world. He has inspired artists and poets down the ages. This is how Shakespeare described the stallion:

Sometimes he trots, as if he told the steps
With gentle majesty and modest pride;
Anon he rears upright, curvet and leaps,
As who should say, 'Lo, thus my strength is tried;
And this I do to captivate the eye
Of the fair breeder that is standing by.'

Round-hoof'd, short-jointed, fetlocks shag and long,
Broad breast, full eye, small head, and nostril wide,
High crest, short ears, straight legs and passing strong,
Thin mane, thick tails, broad buttock, tender hide:
Look, what a horse should have he did not lack,
Save a proud rider on so proud a back.

Standing still, stepping out, or galloping on the racecourse, or even as an unbroken colt, the stallion is always a glorious sight (64, 65, 66).

Such is the aesthetic pleasure to be found in a stud – the stallion, the mares and foals, the youngstock – that people are easily carried away. Sentiment, too, comes into it. A favourite pony, or an old hunter, is retired, being no longer fit to ride and there is a natural desire to 'have a foal from her'.

63 Royal Palace at stud

64 Superb Arab stallion

65 On parade – a French stallion

But one should be cautious. First of all – can one afford it? Breeding from a mare is not cheap. There is the stallion's fee, which even if reduced by using a not too well-known stallion, can still amount to quite a lot of money when you have added the cost of the keep, the travel and so on.

Then there are the eleven months before the foal arrives. During at least five months of this period the mare will have to be fed and properly kept in: there is the forage, the bedding – and the substantial veterinary fees. There are then the years before the foal is old enough to be sold.

Has one the room? A mare and foal (67) will need at least two acres, probably divided into two enclosures so that one part can always be recovering, kept fresh. A proper water supply is often overlooked. All these things are important and should be taken into proper consideration before one decides to breed from a mare, let alone start a stud, which can be very expensive indeed.

The rewards, of course, can be great. One might be lucky enough to breed, if not another Nijinsky or a horse that makes an Olympic team, a Champion show pony or a successful show jumper.

66 Young colts enjoying themselves

67 Mare and foa

68 William Steinkraus (USA), Olympic Gold Medallist

SPORT

Show jumping

Few sports have so increased in popularity in recent years as show jumping. It is very much the 'growth' sport in many countries. This is due to a number of factors. First, far more people can afford it than in the early days of show jumping. Indeed it has long ceased to be an exclusive sport. As a result – and because the Pony Club provides a constant reservoir of young riders – there is no shortage of aspirants for top honours.

Secondly the fame and successes of leading riders all over the world has acted as a great stimulus. Riders such as William Steinkraus, the Olympic Gold Medalist (68), David Broome, the World Champion (70), and Marion Mould (71), a previous world champion and silver medallist in the Mexican Olympic Games on her remarkable pony Stroller, which she actually rode as a child, have all caught the imagination of countless thousands of young people who have taken up riding. Their one desire is to emulate these heroes. Others have been almost equally successful: Harvey Smith (72), Alan Oliver (74), Peter Robeson have all been remarkably consistent over a number of years; and in any sport it is consistency that really counts. If there is any doubt on this score one has only to think of Wilf White (69) and Ted Williams (73), both of whom were going strong before the war; the former was later to become so famous with Nizefela, the latter with Pegasus, and more recently with the South American horses bought for his patron Mr Smith.

70 David Broome (GB), one of the greatest show-jumpers, a World Champion, a European Champion, Olympic Bronze Medallist

69 Wilf White – Olympic veteran

Today's heroes include Caroline Bradley (75) and Eddie Macken (77).

It is consistency again that has made Gonda Butters the leading rider in South Africa. She first became famous when, only fifteen, she rode in adult classes on her famous little horse, Gunga Din. In show jumping, as in any sport, there will always be flashes in the pan, riders who produce one horse which reaches the top and then, once that horse is past its best, are heard of no more. But the really great rider goes on with a variety of horses. Kevin Bacon (78), the Australian rider, is a good example of this, as are his compatriots, Bill Roycroft and John Fahey, who was only beaten by Peter Robeson in a jump-off for the bronze medal in the 1964 Tokyo Olympics.

There is no better example than the d'Inzeo brothers from Italy, who have stayed at the top of the tree for over twenty years. Both took part in the 1948 Olympics and both incidentally have showed their versatility by representing Italy in Three Day Events as well as in show jumping. But even they, like everyone else, can get into difficulties (79), however great, however famous they may be! So the young rider should never despair (76). There is a long way to go, all sorts of troubles to be met on the way, but if a rider has the skill and the determination he, or she, will get there – and the really great will stay there.

71 *Marion Mould (GB), Olympic Silver Medallist, on Stroller*

72 (left) *Harvey Smith, another leading British rider, riding Summertime*

73 *Ted Williams – evergreen veter*

74 Alan Oliver – at the top for twenty years

75 Caroline Bradley, Britain's most consistent lady show-jumper, winning The Wembley Puissance on New Yorker

77 *Eddie Macken on Pele*

78 (left) Kevir Bacon, Australia ace

79 Trouble for Raimondo d'Inz the great Italian Olympic rider

80 *Mary Gordon Watson, World and European Champion*

Three Day Events

In some countries the Three Day Event is almost rivalling show jumping in popularity. It does, of course, offer a tremendous challenge, consisting, as it does, of three phases. On the first day there is a dressage test, not very difficult but fairly demanding. This ensures that a horse has been properly trained, is well schooled, is supple and obedient.

On the second day comes the cross-country: this consists of several miles of roads and tracks to be taken at a steady pace, a steeplechase course of two to two-and-a-half miles and ten or twelve fences, and finally the cross-country course, about four miles long, with some thirty solid and very imposing fences.

On the third day all those horses who have survived so far and have been passed fit in the veterinary parade, have to do a show jumping course to show that after the ardours of the previous day they are still fit, supple and obedient.

Originally this event was a form of Cavalry training. Now it is probably the severest test for horse and rider in the world and only horses of great courage and riders with no less courage are likely to succeed.

The reigning world champion, surprisingly perhaps, is the youthful, attractive Mary Gordon Watson, who not only won the World Championship held at Punchestown in Ireland in 1970, but was also the winner of the European Championships held in France the year before. On each occasion she rode the great horse, Cornishman V, which her father had originally bought in Cornwall as a hunter (80).

In the Mexico Olympics, Cornishman V was ridden by Richard Meade, Mary acting as a girl groom! In the World Championships Richard Meade rode The Poacher and won the silver medal. The Poacher had already been in the winning team in the previous European Championships, so he can probably be considered the leading Three Day Event horse (81) of his day.

Equally famous is Princess Anne's husband Captain Mark Phillips who, on Maid Marion, won the Raleigh Trophy at the 1973 Burghley Horse Trials (84).

There is no doubt that in eventing experience counts a great deal, and few are more experienced than the captain of the Australian team, Bill Roycroft, also an international show jumper (82). But though experience is important, skill and dash play their part and it is for this reason that eventing has become so popular all over the world among young people (83). A rider of great promise, for instance, in New Zealand is Suzanne McCrea (85). Younger still is twelve-year-old Vicki Ketching (86) – all of which shows that you are never too young to start. In Britain the Martin Birds are outstanding young riders (88), but as well as being young and attractive, they also have to be very tough, for they meet tremendous obstacles and all sorts of hazards (87, 89) – which is why this particular sport is such a challenge.

81 Richard Meade, holder of three Olympic Gold Medals

82 Bill Roycroft, the great Australian Olympic veteran

83 *Margaret Shepherd, leading lady rider in Australia*

84 Captain Mark Phillips on Maid Marion

85 Suzanne McCrea, from New Zealand

86 Only twelve, but riding like a veteran

87 Youth no deterrent

89 Anxious moment at Badminton

88 Angela Martin Bird, one of Britain's most consistent 'eventers'

Polo

Many people thought that polo was a dying sport after World War II. However, a small number of enthusiasts in the United States and in England, including H.R.H. Prince Philip, Duke of Edinburgh,

90 Ponies ideally suited for Polo

91 Polo pony hea

who is President of the Federation Equestrienne Internationale (FEI), saw to it that polo was started up again; since when it has become increasingly popular. It is one of the fastest games in the world.

England is perhaps at a disadvantage, as the ground is so often wet. This is, at least, one of the reasons why, whereas only some four hundred people play polo in England, no less than four thousand play polo in the Argentine. With 140 Polo Clubs the game is making a strong recovery in the USA. The Pony Club is also taking up polo all over the world and more and more young people are starting to play (90, 91). The idea in introducing it was to provide something that would be of interest to boy riders, as in most countries the Pony Club is dominated by girl riders.

For the same reason the 'tetrathlon' (sometimes called a 'quadrathlon') has been introduced, which in addition to riding includes running, swimming and shooting. This, like polo, will, I am sure, appeal more and more to boys in their teens who are inclined to find ordinary riding, dressage, even eventing, a little bit 'sissy'.

Racing

Racing has been described as the Sport of Kings. This is not surprising as ever since it started in England, with 'matches' organised by King Charles II on Newmarket Heath, it has been patronised by members of the British Royal family, in particular the monarch of the day. It was, in fact, Queen Anne who founded Ascot Races.

It would be a mistake, however, to think that it is only the aristocracy and the wealthy who like racing. Far from it. Except for football it is almost certainly the most popular sport with the English public, and its popularity grows yearly all over the world.

This in part is, of course, due to the enthusiasm for gambling, because racing is nothing if not a medium for betting. But as most gamblers have learnt to their cost, it is a good deal easier to lose than to win. It is probably true that the majority of those who bet are not really very interested in horses. But fortunately there are plenty of people who are, and they get as much pleasure from seeing a good horse run, or even just parade in the paddock, as from owning one or training one or even riding one.

One of the great advantages of point-to-point meetings – races organised on an amateur basis by hunts – is that they provide opportunities for young people to get race-riding experience. Point-to-point meetings also give a chance to lady riders (92): often the ladies race is the most popular in a point-to-point programme. (Since late 1968 women have been licensed as jockeys in the United States.)

A great many leading steeplechase jockeys first learnt the art of Race-riding in point-to-points (93). But many, of course, have no great ambitions to ride in the more demanding steeplechase races, in which they will come up against the top-class professionals. They prefer to stay in point-to-points, and some of them stay there for a very long time. It is not unusual to see a rider of over sixty riding in a point-to-point.

Apart from the actual racing a point-to-point has a wonderful atmosphere, and each Saturday through the season point-to-points draw large and enthusiastic crowds (though in the United States the sport is enjoyed primarily east of Mississippi). For many Englishmen a local meeting is very often their first introduction to racing of any sort, and so point-to-points can be a nursery for race-goers as well as race-riders.

It will be a sad day if ever point-to-pointing disappears – which might well happen if ever hunting were stopped, as all point-to-points are hunt meetings.

The standard of riding may not always be very high, but the dash and the courage and the enthusiasm is undoubted. Moreover it is a wonderful schooling ground for young horses; many future stars are first tried out at the local point-to-points. Indeed many of the top-class steeplechasers, even winners of the Grand National or the Maryland Hunt Cup, have started their racing life in point-to-points. It is the natural progression.

The other stepping-stone to top-class steeplechasing is hurdle racing. From the jumping point of view hurdling is much less demanding than steeplechasing; on the other hand it is very much faster than steeplechasing. For this reason horses frequently migrate from Flat racing to Steeplechasing via hurdling. There are not many races on the Flat suited to older horses, so if a Flat race horse has not established a high enough reputation to justify his standing as a stallion, he is frequently gelded and put to steeplechase racing.

92 Point-to-point: the Ladies' Race

93 *The Open Race*

Hurdling is the ideal introduction (94, 95) – in theory. Often, however, these hurdle races attract enormous fields, many of them discarded Flat race horses, others being young horses who are getting their first experience of the race track. It is not always a very happy first experience because there may be as many as thirty runners, all racing down to the first hurdle at about thirty miles per hour, a truly unnerving experience for any young horse – or rider!

This problem has given the authorities many headaches, but no solution has really been found. Yet in theory hurdling is the ideal link between the Flat and steeplechasing and the ideal introduction to racing for the novice.

94 Fighting it out at the last hurdle

95 Over the sticks at Cheltenham

It is understandable that hurdle races should always be better filled than steeplechases. Apart from the ex-Flat race horses (and today many horses still in training for the Flat take advantage of racing all the year round to help earn their keep), more horses are now bred for speed than for stamina. This is because there is so much more money in Flat racing: not only is the prize money much bigger, but there is the great stud value if a horse is successful. Consequently racehorse owners always hope that they may be owning a real money-spinner – another Nijinsky (103).

In England no Flat race, except the Newmarket Town Plate (in which lady riders can compete) is more than two-and-a-half miles; and only a few, including the Derby (a mile and a half), are longer than a mile. In the United States distances range from five furlongs to two miles. But in steeplechasing no race is shorter than two miles, some being over four miles. The Grand National is four-and-a-half miles.

Despite the fact that there are far fewer horses in training for steeplechasing than for Flat racing, it is a wonderful sport – the 'winter game', as it is known in England (though now it starts in August and goes on right through to the following June). In this country steeplechase races are held under 'National Hunt' rules.

For many people there is no more thrilling sight in the world than a field of magnificent-looking, great-hearted steeplechasers hurling themselves at the formidable obstacles on a winter's afternoon (96, 97, 99). As a rule they are not so elegant as their flat racing cousins, because they are not usually thoroughbred (100), though with prize money improving more and more thoroughbreds are coming into the game. These splendid horses have progressed from the hunting field, through point-to-points, then into hurdle races or hunter chases. In 1969 the winner of England's Cheltenham Gold

Cup, What-a-Myth, had earlier in the season been running in hunter chases and had been regularly hunted in Leicestershire.

From the betting point of view steeplechasing will never be as popular as Flat racing because, with a large number of fences to be successfully surmounted, it will always be too big a gamble. The hottest favourite which has never been known to fall can always be brought down by a falling horse or by a loose horse that has already fallen.

24
13

It will, however, be a sad day if ever English National Hunt racing simply consists of Hurdle races, as has been suggested. Those who advocate such a move are in all probability only interested in racing from the betting point of view, because over the easier fences there are far fewer falls. (It should, however, be added that as a rule a fall in a hurdle race is a far worse fall than one in a steeplechase because of the greater speed, and in all probability the larger-sized field.)

Hurdles, though they are quite high, knock down very easily, while steeplechase fences, though they are higher, generally slope away from the take off and a horse can brush through the top foot or so of the birch. The exception, in Britain, is the Grand National where the fences are much more solid: and bigger, too, which is why it has become the Blue Riband of National Hunt racing.

Steeplechasing does not always consist of big brush or thorn fences with guard rails, an open ditch and a water jump. In the United States often many of the fences are of solid timber, as in the Maryland Hunt Cup (98). This famous race is the equivalent of the English Grand National. One of the most remarkable achievements ever recorded in steeplechasing was the victories of Tommy Smith and Jay Trump in both the Grand National and the Maryland Hunt Cup. Though American-owned and American-bred horses have won some of the most important races it is rare for a horse raced in America to win in Britain. The last American horse to win the National before Jay Trump was Battleship.

In the United States Harness racing is particularly popular (101). Trotting is also practised in Australia, but in Europe the only country to be at all keen on the sport is France. Although Trotting supporters are certainly second to none in their wholehearted enthusiasm for the sport, it has to be admitted that it is Flat racing that is the most

97 *The most famous steeplechase in the world – the Grand National*

popular. This is partly because of the betting but it is largely due to the fact that the Flat race horse, the thoroughbred, is the most beautiful animal in the world.

During the last quarter of a century a number of superb horses have caught the public's eye by their consistent achievements and later by their success at stud – horses such as Hyperion, Ribot, Royal Palace (63), Petite Etoile, Ballymoss, Sir Ivor, St Paddy, Park Top, Northern Dancer to name but a few.

98 The Maryland Hunt Cup

99 Ten Up clears the last fence of the 1975 Cheltenham Gold Cup, just ahead of Bula

2

It is almost impossible to estimate their value. It all depends, of course, on how successful they are at stud. A horse may be the fastest horse in the world, but it does not necessarily mean that its speed will be reproduced in its progeny. To pay a big price, therefore, for a yearling, basing its value almost entirely on its breeding, is a big gamble. It may never win a race. Similarly to pay an enormous price for a successful horse on its retirement, or to buy a share in it can turn out to be a pig in a poke.

The great names listed above – the giants of the turf – represent the glamour in racing; but behind it all is an enormous amount of hard work. Races are won as much in the stables and on the home gallops as on the racecourse (103, 104). The talented and successful trainer leaves nothing to chance: he knows personally the exact requirements of every horse in his yard, as regards both its food and its work.

Many good horses have missed the limelight because they were never fortunate to get into the hands of a top-class trainer. Conversely, a good trainer by his skill and knowledge can win races with moderate horses, not only by the way he can get the very best out of them, but also because he knows how to choose the most suitable races for them.

There is, as a rule, no shortage of youngsters wanting to work in racing stables, though the work is hard and the rewards poor. There is always the hope that one day they might become leading jockeys, or have a yard of their own. Meanwhile there is always the reward of a job well done, and the joy, for so many people, of working with horses.

Trainers appreciate the value of good 'lads', for there is no doubt that a horse reacts to the mood and temperament of its handler. I

100 A fine three-quarter bred steeplechaser

101 American Harness Race

3

103 On the gallops

102 Nijinsky, with Lester Piggott up

104 The string returns to the yard

always remember my astonishment the first time I saw thoroughbred racehorses, only two and three years old, being ridden by their boys to the racecourse through all the Johannesburg traffic. The equable temperament of these stable lads communicated itself to these young racehorses, who reacted by being equally calm and docile (105). In other, more excitable hands they would have been completely unmanageable.

Obviously it is vital for a horse to get on well with its rider: a good jockey will get the last ounce out of his horse – or settle it down, thus preventing it wearing itself out with fretting and sweating. Equally a good groom will keep a horse happy in stable, feeding well and relaxing, whereas a bad groom will worry or even frighten a horse, so that it becomes a difficult horse to muck out or feed. Such a horse is going to be a problem to any trainer, even the greatest. If wise he will get rid of the groom.

105 The race is over and they make for home

Hunting

It has often been said that all competitive equestrianism stems from hunting. This could well be true, for it is the oldest equestrian sport in the world. It is surprising, however, that it should not only have survived into the twentieth century, but should have increased in popularity. Today in Britain there are few parts of the country that are not the territory of a pack of hounds. In all there are well over two hundred packs and most of them are well supported, with fields of anything between fifty and a hundred mounted followers, and considerably more in some parts of the country on a Saturday (106).

Even more satisfactory in Britain is the strength of the Hunt Supporters' Clubs, which most hunts now boast. These consist of people of all ages and all walks of life who follow the local hunt in car or on foot. These Clubs play an important part in two respects. Firstly, they provide useful funds, raising money by various means, from Whist Drives and Draws to Terrier Shows and Gymkhanas. Secondly, by broadening the basis of support for hunting, they give the lie to the old criticism that hunting is an exclusive sport, only enjoyed by the privileged classes, and at the same time act as ambas-

106 Part of the pageantry of England

sadors for the sport, demonstrating that hunting can be a sport enjoyed by all sections of the community.

It is not easy to analyse the reasons for the popularity of hunting. In the early days in England the interest lay entirely in the ancient art of venery. Many centuries ago man started breeding packs of hounds to hunt a chosen quarry. This provided great fascination too for a countryman or naturalist – as indeed, it still does today.

In the eighteenth and early nineteenth centuries two important developments took place. The first was the gradual enclosing of land that had hitherto been open spaces – common land, heaths, marshes even. The small enclosures, or fields as we know them today, meant that if hounds were to be followed fences had to be surmounted. Followers to hounds quickly discovered that this added to the enjoyment and so the riding became as important an aspect as the hunt itself or the hounds: but not yet more so.

The second development arose out of the gradual redistribution of wealth caused by the industrial revolution. Many, many more people could afford to hunt. In the mid-nineteenth century it became the 'in' thing to be a follower of hounds. Membership of a hunt became a social passport, eagerly sought by many at that time. Consequently the size of the fields – the followers, not the enclosures – grew enormously. It was not unknown for the more fashionable hunts in Leicestershire and the Midlands to have fields of six hundred or even more. Obviously only a mere handful of these great numbers were primarily interested in the hounds. With such large numbers, most of the field would be so far behind the hounds that they would not even see them. Consequently the emphasis in hunting shifted. People went out hunting because they loved riding, galloping and jumping. The hounds, obviously, provided the sport, but few were any longer interested in the ancient art of venery.

107 *Hounds and field move off from the meet*

108 *(overleaf) Rugged country near Auckland*

109 Superb setting for hunting in New Zealand

One likes to think that in the twentieth century the pendulum has swung back: not, of course, completely to the days when the whole emphasis was on the hounds, but certainly away from the days when the interest was entirely in the riding. This is not a little due to the Supporters' Clubs and, of course, to the traditional love of hunting among country-dwellers, for whom the winter would be dull indeed were there no hunting(107).

Hunting also flourishes, of course, in many countries other than Britain. In the United States and Canada it is, perhaps, still a little more exclusive than in Britain, where since the war hunting has become so much more democratic.

I am not, I think, being altogether insular in suggesting that the British Isles are more ideally suited to hunting than any other country – the climate, the terrain, the conditions generally. But this does not mean that hunting is not carried out in most attractive conditions all over the world – in New Zealand for instance, where the grand rolling countryside makes for wonderfully attractive sport (109) and hazardous excitement is provided in the more rugged areas (108). Much the same conditions prevail in Australia. Despite a certain artificiality, hunting in these countries fulfils a genuine need for large numbers of people.

In Southern Africa it does even more. The jackal in this part of the world is a very real threat. The only way to remove this menace is through the hunting of the jackal with a pack of hounds (110). In South Africa landowners can be fined if they refuse to allow hounds on their farms or estates. A good many hunts would doubtless welcome similar conditions in Britain, where owing to a more intensified agricultural policy and a more stringent economy it is not every farmer who welcomes the hunt on his land – especially if

110 The Rand Hunt Club

it is wet, or in spring when he is lambing and the wheat is coming through!

Nevertheless hunting, anachronistic as it may be considered, flourishes as never before, with new recruits joining in almost

embarrassing numbers. Admittedly, hunting has problems, which will certainly increase rather than diminish in the last quarter of the twentieth century, but I believe that these problems will be overcome.

The Rodeo

Of all the forms of sport and entertainment, to which horses contribute, there could perhaps be no greater contrast between the traditional elegance and poise of circus Liberty Horses (112) and the dare-devil excitement of the Rodeo. Some of these astonishing action pictures of the Rodeo may well make one wonder if this is really sport (111, 113), but in fact, especially in the American West, it is tremendously popular.

In quite small towns a rodeo is held every Sunday and all the hands turn out to try their skill either at riding a bucking bronco or at 'roping' (114). A calf or a young cow is loosed into the arena and the 'roper' has to lassoo it. The winner is the one who does it fastest. There are all sorts of variations of roping, but they are all entertaining – even if a little exhausting for the calf: in a single day a calf or cow will be roped many, many times.

Much of the credit in roping obviously goes to the horse, and a roper will spend long hours training his horse which has to be capable of great bursts of speed and sudden turns. Once a horse and rider work as a team they are capable of great success and will soon get into the top-class performances of the bigger rodeo.

111 *Skill and entertainment of a very different kind*

Quarter horse competitions are extremely popular and they demand the highest skill in horse and rider. The Quarter horse is considered to be the oldest breed of horse in America. It originated in the Carolinas and Virginia, well over three hundred years ago. In those days races consisted of matches of about a quarter of a mile – hence 'quarter' horses – and these agile little horses were unbeatable over these short distances. In addition they are thought to have exceptional 'cow sense' and are therefore ideal for rodeo events such as cutting (singling out one beast from a small herd), roping, barrel racing (bending) and bulldogging (when the rider throws himself off his horse on to a young bull).

Better known, at least by name, is the Mustang, or more accurately the Spanish Mustang, which is descended from the horses brought over by the Conquistadors, migrating through Mexico to the United States. Many of these Mustangs were captured by the Indians and so they became traditionally associated with the Indians; others proved to be the foundation for many breeds of American horses. Some are still wild; but they are hunted for dog-food and are in danger of extinction.

In parts of the West the rodeo is the most popular weekend sport and the man who is successful is a local hero, especially if he is as good at riding a bull (115) as he is riding a horse. Riding a bull has been described as the most dangerous of any major competitive sport. The rider is only expected to stay on the bull for eight seconds, but, in addition to courage and toughness, he also has to show finesse and style if he is going to win. It is hardly surprising that they are supposed to be 'tough, mighty tough, in the West'.

12 *The celebrated Schuman Liberty Horses, from Copenhagen*

113 *Better him than me!*

114 *Skill by both horse and rider*

115 *'They're tough, mighty tough in the West!'*

Conclusion

The pictures in this book show the enormous amount of pleasure that horses and ponies can still give. But one should always remember certain very important things about the horse if one is going to fully understand him.

In the first place he was, originally, a herd animal. Man has removed him from the herd, so, in a sense, he is permanently lost. One sees evidence of this every time one puts a horse into a field. Immediately it trots around, instinctively looking for the rest of the herd. In a different way it is noticeable how a pony does not like leaving the collecting ring at a show or a gymkhana. In this case it is reluctant to leave the rest of the herd.

Away from the herd a horse has a different personality. With the herd it acts instinctively: it gallops, turns, grazes, lies down, bucks and kicks, according to the behaviour of the rest of the herd. But without the herd it is dependent entirely on the will of man. It is for this reason that it allows itself to be controlled by man despite its superiority in weight and size, strength and speed. It is as though it is saying, 'You have taken me away from my herd; therefore, I am entirely in your hands: it is up to you to tell me what to do. I trust you.'

What a responsibility for man. This great and wonderful animal has put itself entirely at man's mercy. It trusts him.

The natural nervousness of a horse or pony is due to this same fact, that without the herd it has only a limited will of its own. It is anxious, uncertain, as is betrayed by its ever-moving ears, trying to pick up any sound or signal. So often a man confuses a horse because he is not definite, cannot properly communicate with it. Away from its herd the horse needs understanding and help. The man who gets most from his horse is the man that best understands it. It is worth a great deal of trouble to properly understand your horse or pony.

The Illustrations

The Working Horse

Riding

Food for Thought

Written by Mary Atkinson
Illustrated by Mike Spoor

My name is Seth. I live in Los Angeles. Some people in my city eat lots of junk food and do little exercise. Many of these people are overweight. Other people are too thin. But some people eat good, healthful meals and exercise regularly. They look healthy and have plenty of energy. I try to be one of those people.

Contents

Look for the **Thinking Cap**.

When you see this picture, you will find a problem to think about and write about.

Sweet Enough

The Big Decision

Dad was about to put some more salt on his French fries. "I want to be a granddad one day," he said, and put the salt back on the dinner table.

"You will be, Dad," replied Carl. "When I get older, I want to have a big family."

"That's great," said Dad. "The problem is my doctor told me I need to change my diet. She said that if I don't eat more healthful foods, I'm at risk of a heart attack or a stroke. She said I need to get serious about eating better if I want to be a granddad."

Mel looked worried. "We'll help you, Dad," she said. "We want you to live to be at least a hundred! And I need to get ready for soccer season."

healthful a food or activity that helps a person be healthy

Mom smiled. "I've got a good idea," she said. "Why don't we all start eating better. That way we can all feel healthier and help Dad at the same time. What's more, we won't have to cook different meals for everyone."

The next day, Mom went to the library. She checked out some books about healthful eating. That evening, Mom and Dad sat at the table. They looked through the books, taking notes as they read. Then they wrote a shopping list.

"Our trip to the grocery store will be very different this week," said Mom.

"Yep," said Dad. "But I'm glad we've chosen so many foods I like—strawberries, fish, nuts, and chicken—yum!"

Changes for Carl

Carl secretly dreaded the new eating plan. The first week was as hard as he expected it to be. He missed some of his old favorites. Mom no longer cooked French fries, hot dogs, and fried chicken. There were no soda drinks, loaves of white bread, or packages of store-bought cookies in the pantry. Carl was pleased to discover, however, that he wasn't too hungry. Mom had baked some healthful oatmeal cookies, and there were plenty of seeds, nuts, and fruit ready for him to snack on when he got home from school. She still prepared the cooked vegetables and fresh salads she had always done.

One evening, Dad cooked fish and rice and made a salad for dinner. Carl was about to start eating when he saw the Jones family from next door pull into their driveway. Ryan Jones was carrying a take-out pizza box. Carl put down his fork.

"I don't want to eat this stupid, healthful food anymore," he said. "It's not fair that Ryan can have pizza for dinner and I can't!"

"Hmmm, I see your point," said Dad. "How about if we have take-out food on Friday nights? If we've eaten healthful food all week, we can take a break on Fridays. That way, we won't feel like we're missing out on some of our favorite foods."

Carl agreed that this was a very good idea, especially since tomorrow was Friday.

Take-out food
is often high in
unhealthful fats.
To feel healthy, make
take-out food an
occasional treat, not
an everyday habit.

Getting Fit

Mel was also finding it hard to get used to the new eating plans. However, she was determined to stick with them. She wanted to be healthy and fit. She knew that healthful eating would help with her soccer training. She also knew that it was much better for her health than dieting. Some people at her high school went on diets, cutting out certain foods. Mel had noticed that they often looked tired and unwell. Even if they lost weight, they soon put it on again afterward.

"Eating right is not about starving yourself," Mom told her. "You will get in shape slowly but safely this way, and the good news is that you will feel great. Healthful eating is something you can keep up for a lifetime."

That evening, Dad brought home a present for the family. He'd been to see his doctor. She had told him that he was already much healthier. However, she had said that he needed to exercise, too. This would help build up his heart muscle. Dad had bought a stationary exercise bike from a co-worker who wasn't using his anymore.

"You can use it, too," he said to Mel. "It will help you train."

Starvation diets make your body think a famine is happening. When you begin to eat normal portions again, your body will store extra fat in preparation for another famine.

Reaping the Rewards

To the children's surprise, things soon started to get easier for them. Carl found that his tastes were changing. Now that he'd gotten used to the taste of whole-grain bread, white bread didn't taste so good anymore. Things were going better for him in school, too. He was fitter and had started doing better in athletics. He even won his first race. He was also finding it easier to concentrate in class. He was getting better grades.

Like Carl, Mel was also doing better in school. Eventually she noticed that she had more energy. She no longer wanted to lie around in front of the TV after school like she had done before soccer season started. Instead, she had joined a drama club and made some new friends.

"I am now trying to encourage my best friend Alex," she told Dad. "Alex has a real sweet tooth. We both used to love eating candy and chips. I am trying to convince her to give up eating so much junk food and to eat healthful snacks instead. I told her that we're both sweet enough already."

Helping Hands

One Monday night, the children walked into the kitchen and heard Dad talking on the phone. He was ordering a huge take-out meal. "Don't do it, Dad!" they yelled. "It's not Friday."

Dad grinned sheepishly, cancelled the order, and sat down. "I had a really hard day at work," he said. "I just want to eat junk food and watch TV."

"We'll help you, Dad," said Carl.

"Remember those grandkids, Dad," said Mel. "Come on, put on your running gear. We'll go jogging. That'll help you feel better."

"I'll help Mom with dinner," said Carl. "I'll make sure we cook something you really love–something delicious *and* good for you."

That night, the family sat down to baked chicken with fresh-fruit salsa, one of Dad's favorite meals.

Dad was feeling better after the run. "This tastes great, kids," he said. "Thanks for keeping me on track. I guess we're all going to have bad days from time to time. Let's agree to help each other when that happens—the way you helped me today!"

They all agreed. After all, it was a small price to pay for everything they had gained.

Put On Your Thinking Cap

Write down your thoughts on these questions. Then discuss them with a classmate.

1. What different benefits did the members of the family get from eating more healthful food and increasing their exercise levels?
2. Why do you think some people find it hard to change their diet and eat more healthful foods?
3. Why do you think Dad suggested that they all help each other?
4. How could you help someone who wanted to eat better achieve this goal?

What's the Problem?

In the past, people cooked most of their food themselves from the basic ingredients. There were few fast-food places, and most meals were prepared at home. People ate very few processed foods. Today, supermarkets are full of ready-made meals, candy, and soda. Fast-food meals are cheap, and many people regularly eat take-out food. These meals are quick and easy. However, they are often high in fat, and they seldom contain as many nutrients as fresh, natural foods. As a result, more people now have weight problems and related health issues than in the past.

Getting *enough* food used to be an issue for many more people in the West than it is today. Children were encouraged to eat and drink body-building foods, such as dairy products, so that they would grow into big, strong adults. Today, food is abundant and affordable in many countries. The issue now is learning how much and which food is good for you.

In the 1950s, most families ate a homecooked meal most evenings. Take-out food and restaurant meals were reserved for very special occasions.

Processed Foods

White flour and white rice are refined, or processed, foods. They have had much of the grain removed. This makes them lighter and easier to eat. Unfortunately, many of the nutrients and much of the fiber have been removed, so they are not as healthful. They can make people feel full at first. But unless people get nutrients from some other source, they soon feel hungry again. This is because their bodies still crave the nutrients they need. If we don't eat enough healthful food, we can be malnourished and overweight at the same time.

Being overweight and unfit are health issues. They can lead to illnesses such as diabetes. In adults, they can increase the risk of heart disease, strokes, and some cancers. The good news is that as soon as we return to a healthy weight, the health risks go down.

Understanding Food

Foods are made up of three main kinds of substance: carbohydrates, proteins, and fats. Carbohydrates are found in foods such as bread, rice, and cereal. They are sources of energy. Proteins are found in milk, eggs, meat, and beans. They are needed to build and repair the body. Fats absorb vitamins A, D, E, and K, and are needed to make things such as hormones. However, some fats are healthier than others. Olive oil and canola oil are healthful fats. Other kinds of fats are unhealthful, especially those called trans fats or saturated fats. You can read the labels on many processed foods to see which kinds of fats they contain.

Healthful Food Habits	Unhealthful Food Habits
1. Eat plenty of fresh fruit and vegetables. They're full of vitamins and minerals.	1. Try not to eat fried or deep-fried foods too often. They can contain large amounts of unhealthful fats.
2. Choose to drink more water and milk, and drink fewer sodas.	2. Remember that the more processed a food is, the less likely it is good for you.
3. Eat more unprocessed grains, such as brown rice and whole-grain bread. They contain more fiber than processed grains. Fiber is good for keeping your intestines healthy.	3. Some meats, such as bacon and sausages, are high in fats. Try to eat less of these. You can replace them with foods such as chicken and fish.

Next time you go to the supermarket with your family, check out the nutritional information on the foods before you put them in your cart.

Figure out which fruits and vegetables you like most. Do you prefer vegetables raw or cooked? Try to eat as many different colored vegetables as you can.

Put On Your Thinking Cap

Write down your thoughts on these questions. Then discuss them with a classmate.

1. Think about the foods you've eaten in the last twenty-four hours. Which ones were healthful? Which ones weren't so healthful?
2. Imagine you are eating out. What foods could you order that would be healthful and tasty?
3. Are there any ways you could improve your diet to make it more healthful? If so, what are they?

The Food Pyramid

A food pyramid is a diagram that shows you approximately how much of each kind of food you should eat. The USDA food pyramid (below) divides foods into five groups plus oils, or fats. The five groups are:

- Grains, such as breads, rice, or oats
- Vegetables
- Fruit
- Milk, including cheese and yogurt
- Meat and beans.

Each group has its own colored triangle on the pyramid. The size of each triangle shows you approximately what proportion of your daily food intake should contain that food group. For example, it recommends that you should eat plenty of grains and just a little oil. If you want to find out what amounts are best for someone of your exact age, height, and weight, log on to **www.mypyramid.gov** and fill in your details. You'll also find more information about the food pyramid at this website.

Studies in England have shown that fish oils appear to help children concentrate better and feel more energetic. These oils contain omega-3, a healthful fat.

To be healthy, a person needs to eat foods from all the food groups. Exercise is also important. That is why the food pyramid diagram shows a person climbing stairs. Children need at least an hour of physical activity each day.

What's Wrong With Sugar?

Sugar is a natural product so it doesn't contain any unhealthful chemicals. However, white sugar is a refined food. It has lost most of its vitamins and minerals. The body digests it very quickly. Large amounts give you a short burst of energy, often followed by a feeling of irritability and tiredness.

Sugar is not a fat, but if you eat too much of it, your body converts it into fat. Many fat-free products contain a lot of sugar, so check the labels. Just because a product is fat free doesn't mean it is healthful.

Food Issues Around the World

Eat Right, Be Bright!

UNITED KINGDOM – School children in Britain have a cooked lunch at school. Recently there have been campaigns to make these lunches more healthful. Research has shown that hyperactivity and tiredness in school children can sometimes be linked to poor diet.

Long Lives Cut Short by Fast Food

JAPAN – On average, people in Japan live longer lives than people in other countries. Their traditional food is very healthful. However, Western fast foods have gained popularity in Japan. As a result, the rate of heart attacks and other diseases has risen much higher than in the past.

Healthful Habits

SWITZERLAND – Many children still go home from school at lunchtime to eat with their families. The lunch break is up to two hours long! Their families can make sure that they get a healthful meal, and the walk to and from home provides the added benefit of extra exercise.

Famine

KENYA – In some African countries, such as Kenya and Ethiopia, droughts can result in famines. Sometimes, just getting enough food to survive is an issue for millions of people. At these times, they must rely on aid from overseas agencies.

More Exercise

CHINA – In the 1960s, just getting enough food to survive was an issue for many people in China. Today, with increased wealth, obesity is starting to become a problem. Children are now being encouraged to exercise more and eat more healthful food.

What's Your Opinion?

Eating healthful food has many benefits! We have more energy, feel happier, can concentrate more easily, look better, and are generally healthier. However, if our friends eat mainly unhealthful food, it can be hard not to eat the same things as they do, especially if they eat foods that we enjoy. It can take time to learn which foods are healthful and to figure out a balanced, healthful diet. It can also be difficult adjusting to unfamiliar foods. As kids, it can also be difficult to eat healthful food simply because often it is other people who choose the menu.

- In what situations are young people able to choose what foods they eat?
- How can young people influence what foods are prepared for them?
- Do the benefits of eating healthful food outweigh the difficulties? Why or why not?

My parents buy most of our food at health food stores. We have always eaten healthful food, and I enjoy it. However, some kids at school made fun of my packed lunch. When I was younger, I used to beg Mom to let me eat what my friends ate. But now my friends are starting to want to eat like my family. They are realizing that it can be tasty and it helps keep me fit and healthy. Eating well is definitely worth it.

I used to eat lots of candy and take-out foods, and I drank mostly soda. I was overweight, and I also developed diabetes. My doctor told me which foods were best and which I should avoid. At first, I found it hard to resist eating the wrong things. Sometimes I would get angry at not being able to eat what I wanted, but my dad helped me through those times. I'm glad I stuck with it because I'm no longer overweight, and my health is much better.

My mom works long hours and picks up easy-to-cook foods from the supermarket on the way home. I don't want to make life harder for her by demanding better food. But I may try to work out some easy, healthful meals that we can prepare together on the weekend and store in the freezer. Cooking food at home is often cheaper than buying ready-made food. Mom may be pleased when I explain that we can save money by being healthier.

Think Tank

1 Think of the advantages and disadvantages of fast food. Do you think eating fast-food meals on a regular basis is a good idea? Why or why not?

2 There are many forms of exercise that don't involve buying expensive equipment. What forms of exercise can you think of that you can do easily and safely?

3 How can you promote healthful eating habits in your family and with your friends?

Index